12:2

ISBN: 1519745524
ISBN-13: 978-1519745521

Please take a moment to write Rusty Boruff your questions, thoughts on the book, or to find out more on One Eighty at;

Rusty Boruff

1518 Washington Street

Davenport Iowa, 52804

Or leave a comment at www.rustyboruff.com

Table of Contents

Chapter 1:
The Struggle

As I rolled up my thin mat off the cold concrete floor, I was struggling to deal with the emotions of another day in jail. Going on nearly a year and potentially looking at 13 more, the stress of being totally out of control took its toll on me every morning. I walk into the dayroom with my sandals to grab my bagged breakfast and sit down on the cold, steel bench. This is what I called home. The open shower shared by 12, the small cell where I slept on the floor because of overcrowding, the tiny TV behind scratched glass, never walking outside, and only receiving visitors through 3-inch plastic. For me, the worst part was the buzzing of the lights that remained on 24/7.

While sitting in my new-called home, I knew I had two options. Let the "time" own me, or "own" my time. I was tired of being a homeless addict. I was tired of hurting people and being hurt. Finally, I realized that maybe God had put me there for a reason. God knows He tried getting my attention for so long but honestly, I was too sidetracked. Finally, I was in a place where I had no other option but to listen. Changing my life didn't start when I got out. It started now.

12:2 is a book that simply was created to help people like me, struggling with life, find a healthy outcome. You may not be in a jail cell right now but you could be at a cross roads and possibly the toughest time of your life. The decisions you make right now will literally affect the rest of your life. In this book, you will find the things that helped me overcome my struggles.

Hope is a reason to change…if we have no hope, do we really have a reason to change our lives? Where are you drawing your hope from now…are you drawing it from your partner, your friend, another Christian believer, or from God? Jesus, in my opinion, gives you the best shot at living a better life; one that's better than the one you're living now. A better life means one that is less painful, less dangerous, and much healthier. More importantly, it means a life of better relationships, freedom, real meaning, and satisfaction. If you want a life more like that and less like yours, then you're in the right place. I can't guarantee you a "perfect, go easy cruise" once you overcome your addiction and habits. However, I guarantee that if you place your hope in God, your life will be changed forever and you will do things you never thought possible!

When it comes to addiction, it's like our walk with Christ; you get better, or you get worse. There is no in between and there is no standing still. You're either moving forward or you're moving backwards. This book is for everyone who wants to grow closer to God and get rid of the things in their lives that keep them from doing just that. Our struggles may be with food, stress, work, drugs, alcohol, porn, anger, resentment, and the list goes on and on.

I don't write this book with some fancy counselor degree or a seminary college background. I draw mostly from my personal relationship with Jesus Christ and my own life experiences. You don't have to be a "Christian" to begin this book, but my prayer is that at the end, you'll know Jesus.

Belief systems cause emotions and feelings which then cause us to act. Usually we overreact or under react, but behind all of our actions are emotions and feelings which are driven by the way we think. Usually this thinking is wrong and it's learned over the years of our lives. One of the purposes of this book is to replace those "false beliefs" with "true beliefs." Don't let your emotions run your life. Let God run it instead.

Romans 12:2 states, "Do not be conformed to this world, but be transformed by the renewal of your mind, that by testing, you may discern what is the will of God, what is good and acceptable and perfect."

Paul the Apostle states that it is by the renewal of our minds that we learn obedience and discernment. Furthermore, it's the conviction and power of the Holy Spirit that breaks our habits and the struggles that torment us on a daily basis. You see, this also comes from Paul who writes, "Why do I do the things I don't want to do?" (Romans 7 paraphrased). **Paul, one of the greatest men of the Bible, struggled just like you and I do, yet he recognized his weakness.** Paul let God's glory shine through it, and he let God's conviction bring correction. Paul then renewed his mind to the spirit of God and not the things of this world.

My Struggles

There was a time in my life when I remember sitting down next to our 10 foot glass table with a few ounces of cocaine spread all over it. I would stuff it up my nose until one nostril would be pouring out blood and then I would switch to the next. After that one was bloody, I would start eating it. My friends would try and pull me back from the table, yelling at me saying, "Rusty, you're going to kill yourself." I would respond that I could quit when I wanted to and I told myself that I didn't want to live past 25 anyways. I would hop in the shower, and as soon as the hot water would hit my back, blood would come pouring out of my nose and even my mouth at times. You see, even through all that, at age of 19, I still couldn't admit that just maybe, I had a problem.

There was another time in my life, after my first few months in jail, when I bailed out. I gave up the drugs and drinking (for the most part), but I still wasn't willing to give up the sexual sin in my life, either pornography or physical lust. I realized, if I couldn't be honest with myself and others and admit it and quit it by sharing my problems with those I needed to, then God would do it for me. Trust me; it's a lot less painful if we do it ourselves. I truly realized that the secretiveness of sin and addiction can be stronger than the sins or addictions themselves. In a sense, **I was addicted to lust and allergic to love.**

Chapter 2:
Welcome to Your New Life

This book will help you repair the foundation of your life. Just as a building needs some repairs and maintenance due to weathering at times, so do our lives, due to the storms of life we weather. It's not easy out there. The drugs in the movies, sex on TV, and alcohol on billboards all cry out for our attention. For me, the only way I can stay sober in this crazy life is by accessing the grace of God. **This book is intended to be raw, in that rawness, I pray you will discover the truth about your struggles and pain.**

We want to create a community; a group of people who share a common problem but also share a common goal. They participate in each other's growth and healing. In this way, each group member has a full opportunity to solve common problems for himself or herself. Every member of the community is there to help each other. You'll be helping each other recover from addiction. We are our brother's keeper. We are responsible for each other. There is no such thing as cruising through recovery or discipleship, keeping your head down, doing your time.

Chances are there are four types of people we will find in our community.

- The Addict: Those of us who are completely addicted to a chemical and there is no criminal activity.

  Functioning alcoholic, drug user, shopaholic, workaholic, eating issues, adult pornography, etc.

- The Addict Criminal: Those of us whose main problem is chemical use, but are willing to commit a crime, because of the addiction.

  A struggling addict convicted of a few misdemeanors, in and out of treatment centers, stealing to feed an addiction or habit, etc.

- The Criminal Addict: Those of us who are mainly interested in crime; however, an addiction is usually present.

  Prostitution, habitual criminals with limited substance abuse, convicted of numerous felonies, etc.

- Extreme Criminal: Those of us completely addicted to crime.

  Child pornography, no substance abuse, dealing, habitual criminals, extreme theft, etc.

Which one hits home for you?

The important part here is not to label yourself something that God wouldn't label you as. If you know Christ and have repented, you're forgiven. No ifs, ands or buts. However, I do believe it's important for you to come to the first step by acknowledging your issues, habits, addictions, and struggles.

Transformation

In my opinion, one of the first steps of transformation is choosing what you desire. How many things in your life do you pursue that you don't first desire? None. You chose drugs, anger, gambling, food, drinking, and sex because you desired to feel better or to relieve stress. You still made the decision to drink, eat, or shoot up. In order to pursue Christ and righteousness, you must first desire Him. It doesn't mean you have to understand it all or that it all needs to make sense. You simply need to be open to it.

The revelation that made the biggest impact in my life at the time was when I realized that I needed to hate the sin I was committing in order to stay away from it. Until I hated it, I found myself going back to it day in and day out. That hate came from a more passionate, loving, desire in pursuit of God. There are two different ways to fight recovery: Offensive or defensive. I suggest taking an offensive role. If you choose to take a defensive role, you're waiting for the temptation to come to you, and then hoping you have the strength to say no to whatever that temptation might be. If you take an offensive role towards recovery, you are declaring that you're going to do whatever it takes to avoid that temptation and to fight it before it overpowers you. I have seen many people lose their sobriety by simply being happy with the status quo and taking a defensive approach.

Just like in a basketball game, you need defense. The problem is that the only way you're going to score and win the game is if you're on offense. It's the same in the game of life; the only way you're going to win is if you play some offense.

The reason most people never get to that offensive lifestyle is because it takes guts to change. It takes risk. Imagine the story of Peter as he walked on water. He never would have walked on water if he didn't first have the guts to take the risk and step out of that boat. See this as a challenge and step out of the boat; step out of your comfort zone and take a risk. The first step in recovery is to get serious. Your life isn't a game at a carnival. **Your life impacts generations to come: your family and your friends. The decisions you make today will change the course of history in your life and will impact eternity.**

Fear can keep people from their destiny and what God has planned in their life. What is important to realize is that on the other side of that fear is a thing called joy. Fear is that smoke screen, but joy is the reward.

In Luke 8:40-48, we read about the bleeding woman. I won't get into the details, but let me say this: Her disease at that time might be something considered like today's swine flu or someone walking around covered in anthrax. They were separated from society, couldn't be married, they were ceremonially unclean, and they weren't allowed to touch anyone. This woman was so desperate for God that she fought her way through the crowd and touched Jesus. At this time, in this crowd, Jesus was the thing. It would be as if my body was covered in anthrax and I ran and gave our President a hug. You see, every person this woman touched would then be considered ceremonially unclean. Therefore, running through the crowd to touch the King was a huge deal. She was *desperate.*

Recovery will not help you if you are not desperate. There are times when we can no longer just sit and wait to get better; we must be desperate and pursue The Healer.

We read the same thing in Mark 10:46-52. A blind man sitting in a crowd heard Jesus speaking to the people. He yelled, "Jesus, Son of David, have mercy on me!" The crowd screamed back at him, "Be quiet!" He then yelled louder. Jesus heard him and approached him. During your recovery, when you are yelling out for help, some may tell you to shut up. Don't listen to them; don't be quiet, yell louder. The person you are yelling for makes all the difference.   Are you yelling at your family or friends thinking that it's their job to help you, or are you yelling out for God, knowing only He can save you?

Here are a few things that are important for all of us to realize before we go further:

- Life is not a party boat; it's a battleship.

- Sin has no authority in our life besides the authority we give it; meaning drugs, alcohol, sexual misconduct, lust, hate, anger, etc. None of these have any authority over your life unless you allow them to control you.

- This is the time to stop lying to ourselves and be completely honest with ourselves.

- No condition is permanent.

Chapter 3:
The Big Picture

It's important for us to see the "big picture." Our little minds tend to look at our current situation, circumstance, trouble or temptation, but never look to see where it fits in the big picture. Think of it like this: Picture a seven or eight year old kid. You're the parent playing kick ball in the yard with your child. The ball accidently goes flying across the street into the neighbor's yard. You live on a fairly busy road with cars going by every few minutes. Your child's first reaction is to chase after the ball. You are left standing there as the parent yelling, "Wait! Hold on! Wait for me! Watch out for cars!" You see, the child sees his/her goal and nothing else. A child sees the ball across the road and wants it. Children don't think about the oncoming traffic and the trouble that is near. If you have children, you will know what I'm talking about. Now relate that to your relationship with God. Waiting on God can get so tiring. We often wonder: *Why isn't God getting me out of this situation? Why am I still stuck in this jail cell? Why did my court case get continued again? Etc.*

You see, we are that child running after our goal (the ball), but we aren't seeing the big picture (the cars/trouble coming). The whole time, God is standing there saying, "Wait! Hold on! Wait for me! Watch out for the trouble ahead!"

Read Isaiah 40. Think about or discuss your thoughts about "waiting on God."

It's important for you to realize that this book, AA, another person, or the best program out there will not save you. Jesus Christ is the only way to complete freedom and eternity in heaven. Put your trust in God who holds all the authority and power in this beautiful world.

There's a great possibility that God will break it down to overwhelming odds at times, just like the story of Gideon, so His glory and power can be shown through any situation.

Read Judges 6 and 7. Then think about or discuss how God took Gideon's numbers from around 32,000 to 300, yet they still won the battle. What overwhelming odds are you facing? Do you trust God in the face of adversity?

Surrender

The biggest thing in recovery, in my opinion, is surrender. Are you strong enough to surrender or so weak you try to resist? You see, today's culture says that surrender is a sign of weakness, yet the Bible says that the only way to freedom is through surrender. As Christians, we give up our "rights." According to Philippians, our only rights are the things God offers us as His sons and daughters. It's still up to us to make that decision. In making that decision, what we are saying is this: "God, I surrender all to you."

Do not be fooled that just because you claim to know God, say you believe in Him, have your Facebook religious views listed as "Christian," or even because you go to church, that you're a child of God. It's easy to say we believe in God, but the question I'm asking is this: Are you allowing Him to BE God? There is a difference. I've always believed there was a God. Look around. Look at the stars, the animals, plants, humans, anatomy, and more. It's easy to believe there is a God, but in my life for 20 years, I never let him BE God of my life.

Your Sin + God's Grace = Freedom.

You may have come to the conclusion that "in my life, I haven't been perfect." As I write this, I'm 23 years old, a felon, and have done my time behind bars. I've experienced just about every drug, sold them, taken them, drank years of my life away, and lived a life of sexual immorality like crazy. I've burglarized stores and homes, and stole from family and friends (and those I don't know). My life was out of control for years. Life was rough. The position you may find yourself in at this very moment is rough, but remember that God paints on a canvas that is much bigger than our little view of life.

Every Christian has a past and every sinner has a future. I tell you a fraction of my story, not because I'm proud of it, but because I believe it's important that we are on the same page. It was hard for my family and friends to forget my past, but even harder for me to forget it. I've realized **there is more to a person than the mistakes he/she has made.** I have done the things the state's attorney said I did, but I'm not the man who he said I was. There is a big difference. You are not your addiction, you are not anger, you are not drugs, you are not sex, you are not misery and you are not pain. You are a child of the living God. That, my friend, is a big deal.

You can't quit anything and you can't stop anything. What changes you is God. It's growing closer to Him, and once you do that, your life is sanctified and purified. The drugs, alcohol, anger, un-forgiveness, and hurt slowly start to leave. God let His own son be tortured and nailed to a cross for your sins.

Imagine your son or daughter: Would it be harder for you to die or for you to let your son/daughter die? That shows the love of Christ. God let His own son die so that we can live in freedom. Think about Abraham as he took his son to the altar to sacrifice him to God. His mind and heart were set on obeying God. Why? Because God told him to, and because Abraham trusted God. Thankfully for Isaac, it was simply a test from God. Abraham passed and God provided the sacrifice. This is a picture of what God did when He provided the sacrifice for our sins. This is your test from God.

I'm not asking you to kill your son or daughter, but I'm asking that you go to God in prayer and see what He is asking you to give up and to trust Him with. Is it fear, an addiction, tobacco, a relationship, _____?

Perspective of a Problem

This doesn't mean you will be perfect, but **God would rather have you run hard after Him and fall, than not running at all.** Just because you try to turn your life around, the scenery may not change immediately. Have you ever driven down the road and on one side, it looks like a storm is rolling in, dark sky, rain and maybe some lightning, but on the other side, it's sunny and 80 degrees? That's life. What makes the difference is the window you decide to look through. Life is that car and you're steering. The direction and destination never changes, but the view does.

Of course, in my life, working with individuals struggling with various addictions, I have seen a lot of tough situations people have had to face. I continually remind them that 99% of their problem is the perspective they have on it.

A few of the first residents who came through our in-patient treatment center dealt with 30 or 40 years of alcoholism. I remember the first few times they relapsed and came home drunk. Most places may have cut ties and kicked them out, but God was telling me not to give up on them. Even after the third and fourth time, God still wouldn't let me kick them out.

After these people continually relapsed, they would come home and argue for hours with me in the kitchen. Some nights, we would be up until 2:00 or 3:00 in the morning discussing their issues. What I realized was, even though they wanted to change and they were growing closer to God, they still had temptations which often won out. When they relapsed, they left with their Bibles open on their beds. So just because we accept Christ and grow closer to Him, it doesn't mean those temptations won't stop coming. That is where God's grace comes into play. Pretty soon, they were sober for one week, then relapsed, then four weeks, then relapsed, then two months, then relapsed, and then they were sober for 6 months, and no relapse. You see, most people give up on themselves and others as soon as their expectations of sobriety aren't met. We skim over the idea of grace. **Grace isn't something we deserve, but as Christians, it's something we have.** At the same time, grace isn't an excuse to sin. We can't let our past determine our future.

Death and Eternity in Hell

You see, on the left, you have your life. Some of us may be Christians; others are not, and you're the only one who knows that. On the right, is eternity in heaven. Below in the valley, is death and eternity in hell. In the middle stands one thing; it's the bridge of life, and it's the only hope for mankind to reach heaven. It's Jesus Christ and the cross that He died on. The cross represents a life with Jesus and a personal relationship with the Creator of the universe. It's not religion, or going to church, but speaking, talking, and chillin' with the one who created you. Where will you spend eternity? You aren't guaranteed tomorrow. Today, right now, this is the time to make a choice. When you walk out of this room, you will walk out a different person. You can either walk out ignoring God's plan for your life or you can walk out as a new creation. It's your call, but either way, you're leaving a different person.

Which person do you choose? Your story starts today. *Welcome to the family.*

<u>NOTES</u>

Chapter 4:
Dealing with Pain and Hurt

When I was a teenager, I had a close friend named Evan. Evan and I played baseball together. We were always on the same team and we shared the same passion. He was tall, I was short, but we made a great duo. He pitched and I caught. He hit homers, and, well, I usually walked. One day after years of our friendship, I remember my mom picking me up from school one night and telling me that Evan had passed away. This crushed me and numbed me. I felt dead inside, but on the outside, I refused to show it until his visitation was over. On the way home, I remember breaking down in the back of my parents' SUV with my brother sitting next to me. I questioned God and I remember the trauma of losing my friend, the first friend I felt close to. I felt that God had taken him from me.

Ever since that time, I couldn't grow close to anyone until I got involved with a thing called Civil War Reenactments. During that time, I met Frank and Jesse, two men who became like father figures to me. I talked to these men almost daily and they taught me to train and ride horses. For the first time since Evan's death, I felt like I was close to other guys. Within five years, both those men were taken from me. One died from cancer, and the other completely just stopped talking to me for some reason. I still find myself calling him, hoping someday he would answer. Once again, after this happened, I began to blame God. I asked Him, "Why would You let everyone I get close to disappear?"

Over time, we learn things that are engrained in our lives. For years I believed the lie that if I got close to someone that person would either let me down or die. Because of that, I lived a life of jumping from friend to friend, but never having that close or best friend. I went from girl to girl and when one got too close, I got rid of her and moved on. I would self-sabotage any relationship that I felt was getting too close to me because of the fear that I had learned through life experiences.

Looking back at it, I now see that I can get close to someone without getting hurt. God allowed those things to happen to me and there is no question He used them to mold me into who I am today. Of course I wish those things had never happened. But they did. I didn't know how to process that hurt and pain until years later. When I finally did, God used Evan, Frank, and Jesse to make a big impact in my life and hopefully others. God can take your mess and turn it into a message. He has a unique way of taking our pain and using it as a megaphone to impact the world and somehow the suffering becomes a servant to our message and is amplified to others.

Write down some of your hurt and pain:

_____

_____

_____

I've always heard, 'It's not what you have, but what you do with what's been given to you.'

Today, Jesus is offering you a life of freedom. Freedom is simply having the right to have something better. It doesn't mean that all your troubles will go away, but that God will be there to walk through them with you. Let me ask you the following question:

If Jesus walked into the room you are sitting in and sat in the empty chair, could you honestly say, "I know him"? More importantly, could He honestly say, "I know you"?

Think about it.

For a long time, I didn't feel like I could come to Christ because I didn't know about grace. **I thought my self-worth was related to my net worth.** I thought I needed to have my life together before I could give it to God. However, I realized that if **God made man from dust, then I think He could make a new person out of my mess.**

Bad Things Happen

Read the story of Joseph in Genesis 39.

In this passage, we read about Joseph and Potiphar's wife. Here is just a little background. Joseph was sold into slavery by his own brothers to Egypt where he spent many years. Pretty soon though, he found himself as an assistant to Potiphar, who at that time was a very important man. The Bible states that God held Joseph in extreme favor and so he prospered in everything he did.

Joseph was a man who cared a lot about his character and his relationship with God. He was intentional about avoiding any bad situations (something we should all do), so he refused to be alone in the same room with Potiphar's wife. One day however, he found himself trapped by Potiphar's wife and he fled out of the room after she tried talking him into sex. Joseph knew what to do but before he could get away, Potiphar's wife grabbed his robe, and he ran out of the room.

Potiphar's wife then accused him of trying to sleep with her and he was thrown into prison. Here you have Joseph, who loved God, and God loved him. He excelled in everything he did and stood above reproach, yet through his life, we realize that bad things often happen to good people. He found himself in a prison cell for years. One day, God gave him the opportunity to use his gift of interpreting dreams. He then rose to an even higher level of influence, and Joseph was second in command in the country of Egypt.

My point in sharing this story is to encourage you that even though you may have a good heart and be a great person and even want to do good, however, it's important to realize that bad things do happen to good people, just like Joseph. By the same token, good things happen to bad people. If we remain in line with God and keep our trust and focus in Him, He will carry us through those tough times, and in the end, raise us to an even higher place (spiritually and sometimes physically).

When those bad things happen, they often lead to a life of resentment and un-forgiveness. Here are two exercises that will help us all overcome those obstacles.

Exercise One: Resentment

Resentment: Any person or thing you hold un-forgiveness towards or dislike towards.

Write down your resentment; how it controls you; how it affects you, and how it affects others.

Resentment	How It Controls You	How It Affects You	How It Affects Others
Ex-Wife	Won't go where she is	Keeps me away from God	Kids don't see love

Exercise Two: Finding Your Reality

Write down two good things and two bad things (try using just single words) about your father, siblings, yourself, friends, etc.)

Person   *2 Good Things*   *2 Bad Things*

_____

_____

_____

_____

_____

_____

It's important that we be honest with ourselves in this chapter. After reading the next few paragraphs, take a few moments and go over what you just wrote and see just how honest you were. Make corrections or additions if needed.

Forgiveness

For me, restoration in relation to forgiveness comes down to this: **How can I expect God to forgive me when I can't forgive my mother, father, brother, sister, or friend?** The Bible clearly states in Matthew 6:14-15, that if we hold resentment and un-forgiveness in our heart, it blocks God's forgiveness in our lives. So in reality, what you are doing is giving control to the very one whom you have un-forgiveness and bitterness towards.

In the physical or secular world that we live in, this idea of forgiveness doesn't make sense. The only way we can operate and live a life that consists of forgiveness is by having a relationship with the Creator. This is where the idea of having a personal relationship with God overshadows any of our works that we do for Him. You can do a lot of great things in life, but without God, what good are they really doing you? I know tons of great people who live in bitterness towards their family because they don't know God. They operate a lifestyle of un-forgiveness.

Part of the 12 steps is taking a fearless inventory of your life. The 12 steps are probably one of the best support groups there is, but make sure you don't make the 12 steps your higher power. What this specific step does is challenge you to look deep into your life. If we don't confess sins or hurts in our life, we will grow accustomed to them. It will be molded into our character, which will then affect who we are. I'm not sure about you, but I don't want to be a bitter and unforgiving person. Have you ever met one of those cranky, bitter people before? The reason they are this way is because they didn't confess hurts, pains, and didn't forgive. Then they grow accustomed to those things. Those bad seeds got buried, and pretty soon, they started to bloom in their character. God's Word warns us not to let a root of bitterness grow in our heart. Why? Because it will produce bad fruit like anger, resentment, and depression

Now that doesn't mean it's easy to forgive or confess certain sins in our lives. Man, there was so much crap deep down in my life that it either hurt to talk about, or I was too ashamed to admit it. However, when I confessed that in my accountability meeting and also at the 5th step, I received freedom. Forgiveness is an amazing thing, and once you receive it, you will understand why it's so important to give it away.

I remember when I was in high school. At the age of 17 years old, a teacher made this remark to me out of anger: "Rusty, if my kids ever grew up to be like you, I would kill myself." He was dead serious.

That one sentence made me lose all respect for teachers and authority. I saw that teacher as my authority and my mind said that authority didn't like me and was disrespecting me. From there on, I ignored any authority and disrespected them even if they weren't harmful at all. It took me years to forgive that man. It also took a jail cell, but finally in cell 121, I decided to write him a letter. I asked him for forgiveness and I also let him know that I forgave him. That opened up a floodgate of love in my life.

Write down a list of people you need to forgive.

_____

_____

_____

_____

Write down people that you need to ask forgiveness from.

_____

_____

_____

_____

<u>NOTES</u>

Chapter 5:
Understanding Ourselves

Are you desperate?

You truly are in charge of your success and no one else's. I hope you find comfort in knowing that if you want to change, you can. Be honest throughout this book; everyone has the ability to be honest. Change is really about choice, so make that choice now.

If you're reading this, there's a good possibility you have had a major crisis in your life. **A crisis is simply God's alarm clock. It's the instance that pushes us to the miracle moment in our lives.** The next time you find yourself in a situation that involves a crisis or a problem just remember 99% of the problem is the perspective that you have on it. It's your choice how you will react.

God made this world out of nothing. Sometimes bringing Him nothing isn't a bad idea. The crisis situations in our lives bring us to our knees, humble us, and take us to a point where we have no other option but to rely on someone much bigger than us: God. There is no situation, problem, or habit that is too big for Him!

Our job is simply to be desperate. Imagine a city that has gone into lockdown mode; where every road, bridge, and highway into the city is shut down. No one is allowed to enter or leave the city. This means that bread trucks, semis carrying food, and any and all of those who could get food into city limits are unable to access needy people. I imagine one of the first things I would do is to run to the store to buy every food item possible. Why is that? Because I am desperate. When was the last time you did something crazy for God? When was the last time you were desperate for peace, love, and joy? We never yearn for those things because we live in a blessed country where we can find all those things in the world even though they are not genuine. Drugs, alcohol, food, and sex all give us false love, joy, peace, and acceptance. But at some point, whether that is in a jail cell, at a church altar, or in our homes, those things fade away and we need to become desperate to reap the permanent fruits that result from a relationship with Christ.

Hosea 7:14 (The Message) says, "Instead of crying out from their hearts, they whoop it up in bed with their whores, gash themselves bloody in their sex and religion orgies, but turn their backs on me."

In our addictions and destructive lifestyles, we often moan and groan from our beds, yet we never cry out from our hearts. Cry out to God; don't whisper. Why is it that we never cry out? Maybe it's because we are never desperate enough?

Are you truly ready to change?

On a scale from 1-10, how desperate are you?

I recognize sometimes people are "too desperate" or "off the scale". Then they enter into depression and struggle with such things as condemnation and guilt.

Life History

It's important to deal with the past. The best way I have found to take an honest look at the past is to go year by year, event by event, and write them down. Be completely honest and open with yourself and don't be afraid to write things down that you have never shared before. It's also important because, down the road, you may come back to this worksheet.

Write down things such as: First drink, first drug use, lost virginity, first time in jail, times of incarceration, start of addiction, death of a relative, death of friends, marriage, divorce, children birthdates, etc.

Age 3-5:

Age 6-9:

Age 10-12:

Age 13:

Age 14:

Age 15:

Age 16:

Age 17:

Age 18:

Age 19:

Age 20:

Age 21-25:

Age 26-30:

Age 31-35:

Age 36-40:

Age 41-50:

Age 51-60:

Age 61-75:

Age 76-100:

Who You Are Now (Discovering Lies)

Do you ever ask, "Why do I do the things I don't want to do?" Paul did. You know that famous guy who wrote most of the New Testament? God doesn't call us to a perfect life but we should strive to have one. The road begins now, not tomorrow. It is not when you get out of debt, not when there is less stress, not when your circumstances or situation change, not when you get out of jail, and so on. No, it starts today, this very minute.

You can't possibly move forward until you realize who you are now. For some, it might be an alcoholic, drug addict, inmate, workaholic, shopaholic, person addicted to porn, and the list goes on. The real question is this: Why are you that person?

What I have come to believe and understand is that we are who we are because we think the way we think, which causes us to do the things we do. Most of us live a life in reverse of what we are supposed to. We live a life that is driven by our emotions, fears, desires, and feelings, not by the Holy Spirit.

Who is your God?

What do you think about most? 1-3, rank them from most to least.

- _____

- _____

- _____

Chances are that those are your gods.

Through the years, we have come to believe things that are simply not true or that are corrupt. This is called the "limbic" part of our brain. Think about it, are we born knowing fire is hot, or is it something that we learn over time?

It's important and vital that we see our identity in who God says we are (true belief system) and not what our environment, circumstances, addiction, friends, or habits say we are. Our identity is not in those things, but God says we are forgiven, and that He has a good plan in life to bless us if we choose to follow Him (Jeremiah 29).

In one word, describe your personality.

_____

In one sentence, describe your struggles.

_____

_____

Character Flaws and Issues

Our addiction and criminal thinking creates habits. Manipulating, deceiving, intimidating, controlling, and violating others has become second nature; it's what we do. These are considered *character issues*. They aren't necessarily addictions but can be the result or the cause of addictions. The next page is a quick exercise that will help you define and decide which character issues you might need to work on. There can be more than one and it's a guarantee no matter how perfect the person is; we all have character flaws.

I have seen and been through a lot of programs that will help you get off your addiction or coping behavior. However, once they see your character flaws, you're immediately removed from their program. Now, I believe we all have character flaws. I believe someone with an addictive personality and history most likely has more severe character issues, but personally, if that individual is willing to work on them, I believe we need to provide grace to that person as he/she works through it.

Write down some of your possible character flaws:

_____

We also need to redefine the unspoken or spoken codes you have formed in your life. Here is an example: The criminal code. Don't snitch and don't back down when confronted.

You may have others rules in mind that are part of the criminal code. Write down your old codes and your unwritten rules

Ex: "Don't snitch out your friend."

_____

_____

<u>NOTES</u>

Chapter 6:
Understanding Our Minds

Who God Says You Are (Discovering True Beliefs)

The addictive mind yearns for the same thing, over and over and over, whether it is gambling, drugs, alcohol, food, sex, money, etc. Our goal is to replace that negative addiction with a positive one.

The beginning of wisdom is recognizing what you don't know. My pastor always taught me that God will not consult your past to determine your future. Take comfort in knowing that if you want to change, you can. The process starts now, no matter if you're in jail, prison, or on the streets. Change starts with a choice you make today.

The goal of this chapter is to replace those false belief systems with true belief systems. First, we must realize behavior is always a result of thinking.

Discovering Your Personality

Protective Personality: A mask that we put on to keep people away, so we don't grow vulnerable, or to protect us from a false notion that people will hurt us. Circle which ones relate to you.

The Bully, The Hero, Needy, Phony, Rescuer, The Super Servant, Confused One, Angry One, People Pleaser

Automatic Behavior

Let's take a look at Automatic Behavior.

Describe something you did that was automatic, sudden, and you felt no thoughts were involved. This is a situation when something happened and you responded quickly.

_____

_____

Run through a memory of that situation in your mind in slow motion. Recall some of the thoughts that took place in your mind.

_____

_____

Given those thoughts, did your reaction make sense?

_____

_____

What could you have thought or done differently?

_____

_____

Thinking: Destructive or Productive?

If you put a dollar bill in a six-month-old's hand, he won't know that he can go buy a pack of gum with it. It takes him years to learn and understand that having money means you can buy things. This is the same with emotions and feelings. You weren't born getting angry when someone challenged your opinion. However, maybe you saw your father do it when you were little so you tried it when someone first challenged your opinion. Pretty soon, you got used to it and you started using it as a defense mechanism. So every time you feel challenged by someone or something, you automatically get angry, defensive, and argumentative. Then it becomes second nature and you don't even think about it. It's just automatic behavior.

Thinking is how we make sense of life. It gives meaning to events, our lives, and relationships. If we see an expression on someone's face, thinking tells us what the look means. It tells us whether the person is happy, sad, angry, or annoyed. We might also hear a tone in someone's voice. Our thinking tells us what it means.

Because we depend on our thinking to tell us what's going on, we like to believe that our thinking does a good job of guiding us. We like to believe that we've got things figured out because that means we will make it in the world. On the other hand, bad thinking is a dangerous, even a deadly trap. Bad thinking creates holes we fall into and can't get out of. Thinking can be our best friend or our worst enemy.

Thinking is like wearing colored sunglasses. We get so used to them that we forget we have them on, yet those glasses make everything look a certain way. If they're dark glasses, things appear darker than they are. If they are colored glasses, everything becomes that color. If we think "me, me, me," you will act "me, me, me." The way we think determines the way we act. Proverbs 23:7, in the King James Version, puts it this way, "As a man thinks in his heart so is he."

Patterns of thinking aren't given to us, they are learned. Therefore, it will take time to "unlearn" these habits and belief systems.

Lies

False beliefs are thoughts that we come to believe over time. They are made by projected or learned lies.

Projected Lie: This is a lie we have come to believe from someone else about life.

For example:

- You have to have *this amount* of money to be successful.

- You need this big rim to be cool.

- You have to reach this certain status in order to succeed.

Learned Lie: This is a lie we learn over time that we tell ourselves and have come to believe.

For example:

- If I don't have name brand clothes, people won't like me.

- If I don't weigh this much, people won't be attracted to me.

- If I don't fight and stand my ground, people will believe I'm a pansy.

Lies (circle the ones that relate to you):

I can't trust anyone; if I'm not in control, it won't get done; I'm a victim; I'm superior; I can't be vulnerable; I'm no good; I'm stupid; I'm worthless; I cannot cope without chemicals; I don't need anyone; my values are in my looks; my worth is based on performance; authority betrays me; I can't change, or _____.

Now list your false belief system:

_____

Has someone told you that throughout your life? If they have circle: Projected Lie

Have you told yourself that, or learned it from experiences? If you have circle: Learned Lie

You can't see thinking; it's something you do that is invisible, but its effects are powerful.

Two people may face the same situation but they may respond in opposite ways. One person may end up hurting someone; the other may save someone's life. The difference is in how they think.

Thoughts arise in response to events. A man cuts in front of you in line. Immediately, your mind pulls out your memory of what you did in the past when you felt angry, mistreated, or disrespected. So you react; what a selfish son of a *$&%&*. He deserves to be put in his place.

Our Thinking Process

Here is how it works:

Event: A man bumps you in the grocery store

Specific Thought: You think, "He did it on purpose and he deserves..."

Behavioral Response: Push him back, argue, etc.

Below you will find the Thinking Project. This is an exercise in which you pick an event, write the thoughts you had before you reacted, state how it made you feel, how you reacted, the belief system you believed, the consequences you got, a better thought you could have had, a better behavior, and the consequences that could have resulted if you had chosen better thoughts and behavior. There will always be problems but how we face them and deal with them is what makes the difference.

Thinking Project:

- *Event:*

  _____

  _____

  _____

- *Thoughts:*

_____

_____

_____

- *Feelings:*

_____

_____

_____

- *Behavior:*

_____

_____

_____

- *False Belief System (Lie):*

_____

_____

_____

- *Consequences of Behavior:*

_____

_____

_____

- *Alternative Thoughts:*

_____

_____

_____

- *Alternative Behavior:*

_____

_____

_____

- *Alternative Consequences:*

_____

_____

_____

<u>NOTES</u>

Chapter 7:
Understanding Our Emotions

Feelings and Emotions

Feelings are powerful. They can destroy our life and happiness. What we don't realize is that our powerful feelings are the servant of our thoughts. We can learn to choose what feelings we have and where they take us. They come on us like waves and sweep us away. Feelings can change our life forever and there is no question that they change our moods daily.

Say your feelings are a jet engine. Aboard are all your family, friends, and your life. And you're the pilot. Who determines the direction of the plane? The pilot. Compared to the plane and engine, the pilot is small. He seems insignificant and invisible. In truth, however, he or she is in charge. Your feelings make loud roaring noises, but your thoughts direct them. You are in control.

The challenge is to recreate our pattern of thinking.

What feelings have you experienced over the last 24 hours?

_____

_____

Did you choose to feel that way?

_____

_____

Many of us who are in recovery have experienced so much hurt in our lives. It's what we do with that hurt and pain that makes a difference. I encourage you not to use the sorrow, pain, guilt, and hurt as an excuse to go back to your old way. Use it as the fire and the reminder of the torment that your old lifestyle brought you. It's hard to move on when you're stuck in the past. As we relive and think about the things that have happened in our life, it's easy to get stuck in that cycle again. Just remember; keep your focus on God. When we lose focus, we lose our purpose and our purity.

You need to make a choice right now. Here are your options; circle which one you choose:

The Future   *The Past*

Now live it.

Patience

Galatians 6:9 states, if we don't give up, we will reap the harvest in due season.

Look at the story of Job. This was a man who was stripped of everything he had. Now imagine your life for just a moment. One day you wake up and your kids die. Then your wife is gone. Then you find out you have no money because of a bank error that can't be reversed. In one day, your entire life is taken away from you. How much patience would you have at that time?

Job was a man who lost everything; family, friends, finances, and his belongings, yet he remained patient. In the end, God rewarded him with even more than he lost.

Patience does not come easy, so do not get impatient waiting on patience! The key to patience (I know it sounds weird) is growing closer to God. I have ADHD so even a small thing like sitting down and reading the Bible is hard for me to do. Sitting through a prayer meeting or even holding still during a service is torturous. However, in the end, God will honor it. In life, **usually the hard thing to do is the right thing to do.**

Desires

Desires: Anything you use to cope, escape into, comfort, or to meet your needs and identity.

Circle which ones relate to you and explain how it controls you, how it affects you, and how it affects others.

Desire	How It Controls You	How It Affects You	How It Affects Others
Money	All Consuming	No friends	Dishonest, stole, lied
Body Image			
Sports			
Drugs			
Status			
Sex			
Food			
Fame			
Attention			
Other			

Fear

Fear: Anything that we are afraid of that affects how we live.

Circle which ones relate to you; how it controls you; how it affects you, and how it affects others.

Fear	How It Controls You	How It Affects You	How It Affects Others
Rejection	Trying to please people	Never myself	No one truly knows me
Loneliness			
Success			
God			
Intimacy			
Relative			
Abandonment			
Criticism			
Poverty			
Failure			
Other			

The way we think determines the way we act. You could spend your whole life trying to fix the way you act, but if you never fix the way you think, it won't do you any good. Utilize this exercise every day. Anytime you get angry, lash out, get frustrated, worried, overreact, or under-react, come back to this worksheet.

There are usually three ways we react in a situation. Fight, Flight, and Freeze.

- Fight: We get angry, defensive, and usually destructive.

- Flight: We run from it. If a friendship takes a bad turn, we just cut it out of our lives.

- Freeze: We grow numb. Sometimes we ignore it; other times we don't know how to act.

How do you usually react? Do you take fight, flight, or freeze?

Another way we react is by self-sabotage. I'm really good at this one. Personally, anytime I do great within an organization and move up in the ranks, I self-sabotage it. Even if I think I might be getting in trouble for something small, my first response is to lie about it, which usually snowballs into something bigger. I then find myself pretty much self-sabotaging my job instead of facing the music.

Another way I tend to self-sabotage is with female relationships. For years, if I felt like a girl was getting too close, I would say, "Forget it; I'm getting out." I would do whatever it took to get myself out of that relationship.

Think of an example of how you self-sabotaged something.

_____

_____

What could you have done differently?

_____

_____

Anger

Anger can change your whole life within minutes. Maybe you knock out someone who is hitting on your girl/guy, say something hurtful to your sister or mom, or you hit your spouse or kid or maybe a cop. Anger can control your life. Usually, angry people don't want to be angry, but they find themselves uncontrollable.

Anger is usually a response to pain. Pretty soon, it becomes normal, and every time you feel pain, you react in anger. Chemically, when you get angry, you release endorphins and adrenaline, thereby diverting your attention from the pain. It's similar to using cocaine.

Circle the way that you feel when you are angry:

Big   or   Small

Right   or   Wrong

Strong   or   Weak

Aggressive   or   Timid

Powerful   or   Gentle

Protecting Your Heart

Something I constantly have to remind myself when it comes to a relationship with the opposite sex is that **I would rather have nobody instead of the wrong somebody.** Never compromise God's standards!

I want to ask you a question. Why is it we let certain things in our home through our TV and computer screens but we wouldn't let them in if they came and knocked on the door of our homes?

What is it that is going through your TV screen or computer screen that God is calling you to give up?

_____

_____

See additional resources and worksheets on page 129.

<u>NOTES</u>

Chapter 8:
Relapse and What to Do With It

Recovery is a process, not an event. God can deliver and He will; however, for most of us, it's an ongoing process to grow closer to Him. It's walking out our deliverance through our relationship with Christ.

Relapse Alertness Scale

In almost every relapse with individuals that I have personally mentored, I have noticed some warning signs just before they relapse. Usually two weeks before they relapse, I notice changes in their attitude and personality. First of all, as a mentor, it is important to know your client's personality, otherwise you can't tell when the individual's personality changes. It's also important as a person fighting addiction to know your personality, or else you won't know when it changes.

This is where a teachable spirit comes into play. Don't be offended (as we talked earlier) when someone challenges you on your attitude. Instead, take it into consideration and prayer. Below, you will find what I call the "Relapse Alertness Scale." This simply is a scale for you and your mentor to review as a way to prevent future relapses by dealing with the issues causing that relapse ahead of time.

Listed below are the steps to relapse, as well as examples of personality changes that may occur. Remember, this can change for each person depending on his/her personality. Sit down with another person (mentor) who knows you well and circle the ones that pertain to you. Any time your mentor or counselor brings these up to you, sit down, look at your relapse alertness scale, and see what can be changed. It works from the top to the bottom.

Recovery: *Attending meetings, identifying fears, reaching out to others, eye contact, joyful, happy, spending time with God, spending time with family, being open, trustworthy, volunteering in community, resolving conflict, _____, _____, _____*

Step 1: *Bored, not sleeping well, gossiping, creating drama, change in weight, breaking promises, isolating yourself, day dreaming, fighting, spending time with the opposite sex, arguing, complaining, _____, _____, _____*

Step 2: *Profanity, worry, fearful, dramatic mood swings, drinking a lot of caffeine, irritable, negative talk, griping, skipping meals, business, lust, not listening, "do it all" mentality, skipping church, not attending meetings, _____, _____, _____*

Step 3: Depressed, panicked, looking at porn, lusting over the opposite sex, sleeping too much (or to little), loss of appetite, thinking of using drugs/alcohol, defensive, can't forgive, irrationality, headaches, obsessive thoughts, superior mentality, intimidation, argumentative, self-abuse, isolation, not returning phone calls, justification, angry, _____,

_____, _____

Relapse: Lying, lost in addiction, spending too much money, giving up, justifying social or minimal use of addiction,

_____, _____, _____

Relapse

It is important to understand that relapse is not part of recovery. However, it can be used as a tool to get better (if it happens). It's also extremely important to understand what situations could lead you back to relapse. Write down the things that you have learned from this book that could eventually lead you to a relapse. Make sure you stay away from those things or prepare for them.

Example:

What events could lead to your relapse?

Can't pay bills, fight with the girlfriend, my baby's mom not letting me see my children, having extra time on my hands, death of friends/family,

What dates could lead to your relapse?

November 11th, when I got divorced (anniversary), New Year's Day, January 9th death of my wife, July 4th, St. Patrick's Day, my birthday, family gatherings,

What can I do to prevent those events/dates?

Let my sponsor/accountability partner/mentor know about them, make sure that I'm busy during those days, make sure that I keep up on my job and stay busy, meeting weekly with my accountability partner and talking to him/her daily.

Your turn:

What events could lead to your relapse?

_____

_____

What dates could lead to your relapse?

_____

_____

What can I do to prevent those events/dates?

_____

_____

It's not what you have; it's what you do with what's been given to you. Being rebuked is a good thing and it's actually cited 91 times in The Bible. Don't resist fear or get defensive when someone rebukes you as long as they do it out of love and care for your best interest. Remember that God disciplines those He loves!

Understanding Relapse

I break relapse into two categories; situational and progressive.

Situational: An event or day that causes an emotional, physical, or mental chain of reaction that leads to relapse. Examples could be a divorce anniversary, holidays, job loss, etc…

Progressive: A continues breakdown over time emotionally, physically, or mentally that leads to relapse. Examples could be deteriorating relationship, financial stress overtime, recurring domestic abuse, etc…

The Daily Check

What I call The Daily Check is simply charting out how you did today. In one column you rank yourself and in the other your accountability partner, spouse, sponsor, mentor, or maybe program supervisor (if you're currently in a program) ranks you. Each day you compare how you did that day. Eventually, if you relapse you can go back to this chart and see if the relapse was situational or progressive. It will help create accountability but also will help send red flags if you are progressively relapsing.

Rank how you felt today. When I say feelings, I mean overall. How your day was at work, if you felt depressed, angry, etc... 1 being the worst and 10 being the best. Once you rank yourself have someone close to you rank how your overall attitude was. You can use this chart each week or make your own. It's important to fill these out daily and make sure you save them.

Your Name: _____ **Their Name:** _____

Date: _____

Day	**Your Rank**	**Their Rank**
Monday	_____	_____
Tuesday	_____	_____
Wednesday	_____	_____
Thursday	_____	_____
Friday	_____	_____
Saturday	_____	_____
Sunday	_____	_____

Dealing with Temptation

In Exodus, we read that sin as a lifestyle will slowly control our lives. I see it like this: If we let sin take a hold of our minds, it will then take over our hearts and if it takes over our hearts, it will take over our lives. Sin is a big deal, and it's important to learn not only God's grace, but also how to say no.

We are fish; Satan is the hook and the bait is the temptation. Temptation won't come to you with big red flags playing a song entitled "Come Get Me, I'm Sin". Temptation comes in forms we least expect. For those of you who have fished, think of the bait that you use to catch a fish. I loved fishing and hunting growing up, and I remember playing in my dad's tackle box as a young kid and getting snagged on a few hooks. I didn't see the hook; I just saw the cool looking bait and lure. The hook was hidden.

List the "hooks" the devil usually gets you with (drugs, alcohol, sex, etc.)

_____

_____

Now list the "bait" he lures you in with (money, pleasure, high school girls, fear, feeling of wanting acceptance, or trying to fit in, etc.)

_____

_____

How to Remain Clean, Sober, and Free

You assume that if you think it, then it must be true. You are probably pretty good at challenging other people's thinking, but not your own. Remember to challenge your thinking before you challenge others.

Confronting criminal or addictive thinking and behavior is not snitching. It's refusing to let your brother get away with the kind of crap that will take him right back to chemicals and crime. Telling the truth about yourself and your history is not weakness; it's a sign of strength and courage.

Every human brain holds immense power and knowledge. It's more advanced than the most advanced computer; the smartest human only uses 3-4% of his or her brain. We have behavior problems because we first have thinking problems. Because we have distorted habits of thinking, our thinking becomes distorted, and then our reactions are distorted because of our thinking.

Thinking Stances

I have character traits such as: Victim, good person, unique (think you're in a class of your own), fear of exposure, lack of time perspective, all in, I use power to control, seek excitement, I think everything is mine

Write the three character traits that relate to you:

1) _____

2) _____

3) _____

Emotion Chart

Emotion	Mild	Moderate	Extreme
Sad	disappointed	gloomy	devastated
Afraid	nervous	scared	terrified
Desire	wish	want	crave
Disgusted	dislike	contempt	revulsion
Angry	annoyed	indignant	furious
Guilty	regretful	sorry	self-hating
Shamed	embarrassed	unworthy	humiliation

Insanity is doing the same thing over and over and expecting a different result.

Extreme thinking is a distortion of an addicted brain. Circle the ones that relate to you:

Over-generalization, personalization, extreme thinking, magnification, minimization, jumping to conclusions, selective focus, concrete thinking, closed thinking, emotional reasoning

Triggers

We all have triggers in our lives. These triggers are things that might lead us back into our addiction.

For example:

Addiction (the struggle): Trigger (what ignites it)

Porn: A cute picture of a provocative girl on Facebook

Alcohol: Attending a family wedding or funeral where there is alcohol

Over-eating: Being home alone watching movie.

Anger: Consuming too much alcohol.

For every addiction in life, there are definitely multiple triggers that send signals to our brain saying, "Drink; it's what you usually do in this situation." It's important to recognize these triggers and put up boundaries and have accountability to stay away from these certain situations.

Write down your addiction and then the triggers for that addiction.

Addiction: *Triggers:*

_____

_____

Accountability

Accountability is one of the most vital things when it comes to recovery, discipleship, and transformation. Accountability is having that "best friend" or person you can tell anything to. This person must be able to challenge you in the deepest, darkest areas of your life. They aren't afraid to ask the tough questions, to challenge your thinking, or ask about your behavior.

This person needs to be someone of the same sex and I would suggest someone who has dealt with some of the same issues you may have had. This individual absolutely must be someone you can trust. This will take time, effort, and prayer in choosing this person. However, it is so vitally important. It is also easy for someone to hide out in accountability. Maybe this person meets with his/her accountability partner weekly, but it's always a shallow conversation about the week where no questions are asked. I've had both types of accountability, and in my opinion, **no accountability is better than bad accountability.**

My accountability partner and I usually meet once a week and we talk daily. We both struggle with the same type of stuff; however, more importantly, we both have the desire to change and get better in those areas. I cannot stress to you enough the importance of accountability. Below is an accountability card; it will be something small that will help you get started.

Accountability Partner's Name   *Wife/Children's Names*

_____   _____

Address   _____

Email Address _____

Scheduled time to meet weekly   *Other times we will call daily*

_____   _____

If your accountability partner is married, consider (depending on situation/addiction) getting permission to ask the spouse how your accountability partner is treating the spouse or family at home. I also suggest getting signed-up for accountability software online (for pornography), which sends your entire list of visited websites to your accountability partner's email. Make sure when you check those websites that you do it together to prevent temptation. Please do not ignore accountability. I can't stress enough the importance of true and pure accountability because it will definitely change your life.

When it comes to accountability, remember this: Each person has his/her breaking point. It's the boundaries you put in front of you that keep you from hitting that point.

Many people want to draw a line and ask, "How close can I get to that line?" I say that if you're asking that question, you are too close. Our goal should be to be as far away from that line as possible. Go ahead and draw the line. That's fine, but don't use it as an excuse to get close to the edge.

During my time in jail, I had a man by the name of Rock, among others, come visit me. I remember very clearly that Rock would put his hand on the window, and I would put mine on his through the window, and we would pray together. You need that type of person in your life. Start praying for the person who can be the start of your support group and God will bring that person to you.

Recovery Schedule

It's also important for you to set up a weekly schedule which includes a daily activity that will help your recovery and faith walk. Make sure you give this schedule to your accountability partner also. I have found that one of the most important things to do is to get plugged into a local church (one church, not multiple), so you have a great support group. Fill out your weekly recovery schedule.

Day	Example	Activity/Time
Monday	small group	_____
Tuesday	12 step	_____
Wednesday	church	_____
Thursday	night off	_____
Friday	accountability	_____
Saturday	bible study	_____
Sunday	church	_____

Good Dog/Bad Dog (Feeding Our Mentality)

There is something else that's important to realize. I call it Good Dog/Bad Dog. Whichever dog you feed the most is going to win.

Good dog examples: encouraging movies, positive music, church, recovery meetings, etc.

Bad dog examples: discouraging music, derogatory videos, bars, etc.

Write down examples of your good/bad dogs; which one will you feed?

Good Dog:

_____

Bad Dog:

_____

Double Bind

Have you ever heard the phrase, "You're darned if you do and darned if you don't"? This saying can be so true in our life time. Write down some "double bind" (darned if you do, darned if you don't) scenarios you find in your life.

Example:

If I quit drinking, I'm going to have to deal with the pain of dealing with my addiction, my parent's death, abuse as a child, and every time I get in a fight with my family, I will actually have to deal with it instead of running to the bar.

Your turn:

Double Bind:

_____

_____

_____

_____

In these situations, always remember **the hardest thing to do is usually the right thing to do.**

<u>NOTES</u>

Chapter 9:
Restoration

Are you ready to take a risk?

We are obsessed with the desire to feel good. We don't feel good without consuming an addictive substance (drinking or drugs) or engaging in an addictive behavior (gambling and rage). So our minds become obsessed with repeating the experience. However, if we can replace that "feel good feeling" with something healthier, let's do it. One of my clients said to me once, "When you walked into the jail, I could just see it in your eyes. There was that glow on your face. Something was different about you and we all wanted that." I never came to faith when I was younger because I didn't think it was possible to have fun as a believer. Wow, was I wrong!

Unhealthy addictions create issues not only with our family, friends, but also our health. **Addiction is a disease.** Addiction is progressive, confusing, and a fatal disease. If you stay addicted, you'll die. Take a moment and think about all of the people who have been affected because of your addiction.

Now, like I have said before, we can find comfort in knowing that if we want to change our lives, we can. The Bible says we are a new creation; a new person once we come to faith. So, if you're at that step, you are considered a new person with a brand new start. If you aren't there yet, it's fine. Now, our goal is to get you back to ground zero or get you up to par.

I recommend you get your Bible and you search for "true beliefs" about who God says you are. Not who your mother or father says you are, not who your friends say you are, not even your religious teachings from the past. Find out who God says you are. This is how you replace those false belief systems.

It's important to recognize our faults, but even more important to recognize God's grace and love for us. Hope is the reason to change and that hope comes from forgiveness. We must put guilt, shame, and depression in our past.

Change takes risk. Are you willing to take a risk today even if you don't know what tomorrow might bring? Admit it and quit it; confess it and address it. Realize our flesh is powerless but the God in us is powerful!

Some of us might experience a conviction for our sins. There are times when I get conviction (feel bad) for something. Three years ago that was second nature to me. Little things, things that aren't even in the Ten Commandments, would convict me! It's easy to feel guilty or shameful over that conviction, but my encouragement is that the conviction you get is simply a sign of the Holy Spirit working in your life. When you stop getting that conviction, that's when you need to worry.

My prayer is that God might bring you some conviction throughout this book, not condemnation (made by man), that you will listen to the conviction, and God will give you instructions on how to better your life.

Process of Restoration

While you continue to try and better your life, you may sense a lot of fear rising up. Fear, in any shape or form, is simply a diversion that keeps us away from joy. On the other side of fear resides joy.

There is a definite process of restoration. It takes time. God is a God of restoration if we have the patience to endure it. It starts with confession; that confession leads to repentance. Then in return, we receive forgiveness. Just as a gift is given, it also must be received. That's our duty; to receive from God.

You Can

As those suffering from addiction, we hear people tell us we can't change. It rang so clearly in my head. Eventually, I ended up in a jail cell looking at 14 years. During my time in jail, it was tough, rough, and scary. I remember the beating on the cell bars and the yells that echoed the halls. I remember crying in my cell, not because I was scared, but because I was lost. My old friends abandoned me. I remember wrestling with God for weeks in a cell and asking Him to take away the pain of a disease I had. I remember the heartache of watching as my soon-to-be baby's mom (and then girlfriend) would drive by on her way to school. We weren't allowed to talk to each other, so for months, all I could do was watch her drive by and pray.

I remember not being able to go outside or leave our eight-man cell for months. I won't forget the no-contact visits, the ramen noodles in the sink, and the small scratched up screen we had to watch. Life in a jail cell was miserable.

After receiving Christ, I found a peace and a hope that grew deep inside. Pretty soon, the pain, hurt, struggles, and addictions left. I started a Bible study group and telling everyone I knew about Christ. I found out I was having a boy in the middle of my sentencing hearing, and my 14 years were reduced to two, with five years of probation and thousands of dollars in fines. I began to find new friends, I was healed of my disease, and God began to rock my world in a good way. I could walk into the court room with the favor of God and the confidence that He was my judge. The judge court-ordered me to a faith-based program and went under what our attorney was even asking for, let alone what the state's attorney wanted.

I'm not saying God will get you out of all your issues or legal problems (if you have them), but He will give you the strength to get you through whatever you're facing, and sometimes He just may take you out of it. None of this was made available to me until I decided to forgive others, like my baby's mom.

Do you have a crisis? **The awesome thing about God is that He allows freedom, but He always maintains control.** Just as Jesus and Barabbas were taken in front of the crowd and the crowd was to decide their fate. In Mark 15 we read that they began to cry, "Free Barabbas and crucify Jesus." This didn't make sense because Barabbas was the known criminal and Jesus was simply a religious radical. God didn't manipulate the words coming out of the crowd's mouth from "Jesus" to "Barabbas." No, He let decisions and choices happen, but He maintained control. That's what God does. We can make our own decisions, yet find comfort in knowing that God always maintains control.

Things to remember:

- Grace is given, not earned. The Bible states its unforced rhythms of grace.

- God never asked us to figure life out, so stop trying to. God's glory and strength is found in your weakness.

Hope in the Face of Adversity

Our discipleship home is where I chose to live in the beginning states of what is today, One Eighty. It was located right on the Mississippi River in Moline, Illinois. If you looked out of my bedroom window, past the crack house next door, you could see a glimpse of the mighty river and if you stood on our porch, you could see clearly the river. During the tough, emotionally draining days in the house (every day), I'd walk down to the river and out on the dock. I would stand there amazed. I could see the river which is so peaceful. I could see the birds flying, geese floating, the huge city lights, buildings in the background, the two bridges connecting the great states of Illinois and Iowa, and I could see the beautiful trees and rocks on the bank of the river. I couldn't help but say, "God, you created this all. A blind man could see how magnificent You are." I'd sit and reevaluate my day. "God, I see You in front of me, in the river, trees, rocks, animals, and buildings. I see You and I know You're there, but where are You in my life today?' I believe that is a question we must ask ourselves every day.

I didn't have a Damascus road experience like Saul/Paul. I got saved in a dirty old jail cell by myself, reading my Bible all because of a praying mom and family. There may be times when it's harder to see God than others. At these times in my life, I have to remind myself that all great things are made by not so great times.

War, drought, disease, murder, rape, sin, prostitution, addictions, demons, greed, theft, and death on a cross doesn't sound like great times to me. However, those not so great times made the greatest, bestselling book of all time; the Bible. **Your situation may not be great, but once again, all great things are made by not so great times.**

Before a child is born, there are first the birthing pains. It's hard, it sucks, and it's painful (so I hear), but those things must happen in order for each one of us to be born. In your life now, there might be some pain, but when you make it through the pain, God will show you the creation that comes from it.

Early in ministry, I went through some pain, like being fired after nine months in my first ministry position, where we housed ex-offenders and the homeless. With no warning my boss sat me down in front of all the men living at the home and forced me to read my letter of termination that she had written. Was that humiliating or what? Not only that, but the ministry and house that I worked so hard to build, the very thing I put 70 hours a week into, where I slept on the floor at night because I couldn't afford to drive an hour back to my parent's house, the thing that I took a 70% pay cut to do, I was not only fired, but kicked off the property immediately, and was notified that I had 24 hours to get my stuff out of there. Let me tell you, that wasn't great day.

What came out of that in the end was a bond between those men and myself. Through a series of events, I was able to move back into the house. The men and I started our own ministry (prematurely, I might add, but it was the only option at that time) and we grew together. One Eighty was birthed out of that situation. That day in July 2009 was a birthing pain to what God had in store for His great divine plan. The pain turned into a gain.

Look at the story of Joseph and the seven years of drought for Egypt. They were told in a dream that there would be seven years of drought, followed by seven years of amazing feast. If Joseph didn't prepare for the drought during those seven years, Egypt never would have made it to the feast. Now, you might be in a jail, at a recovery home, or you just might be in a place of desperation. Now is the time to prepare. This is the seven good years God intended for you to study, read, pray, and to build your faith. That way, when the sickness, pain, temptation and struggles come, you are prepared to face them.

I sat in jail for months wondering why I was there, but I realized that if it wasn't for that time in jail, the time that I decided to prepare, I never would have made it through the hard stuff later on.

Communication

Communication can destroy or build a relationship within seconds. I've been through the 12 steps for many different reasons including drugs, alcohol, sexual addictions, and anger. The most challenging and rewarding for me was when I went through it for texting. People have a tendency to pull things from a text message that they may not in a person-to-person communication.

When I text, I can say a lot more and be a very bold person. This can be good or it can be bad. The one thing that the person can't receive in a text or email is the heart of the message. It's impossible.

The other thing I want to touch on is conflict resolution. I have the type of personality that wants to run in the other direction if I hear "conflict." Conflict truly runs my life. I don't answer my phone, then I worry about not calling them back, then people get mad that I don't call them back, then I never call them back, and it's a vicious cycle. It's a vicious cycle all driven by fear of conflict.

One thing that is a constant struggle for me personally, and that is a learning process for me continually, is conflict resolution. I hate to break it to you, but you will have conflict in your life. How you deal with it is what makes the difference.

I remember after I was surprisingly fired from my first ministry position, our pastors gathered a group of people in our conference room. It was my accountability partner, a close board member, two of my pastors, my old boss, and three of her board members and friends, along with me. During this time, I experienced firsthand how to handle conflict. During that meeting, deep down, all of us knew that we would leave that meeting agreeing to disagree. But wow, what we realized was that there was so much miscommunication that led to me getting fired. It was the main reason that my job prematurely (in human eyes) ended, all because of a lack of communication.

We started with my boss stating her side and then I stated mine. Then we opened it up to her and the board members, and then it went back to me and my board members. The pastors were simply the mediators in that situation. Of course, even typing about it brings a gut wrenching feeling in my stomach. However, the amazing thing that I learned from my pastors in that meeting was that, even in conflict, God can get glory. We left that meeting with an understanding that we disagreed but that God can still make a message out of our mistakes and miscommunication.

Excuses

Luke 14:15-24 is the story of the Parable of the Great Feast. In this parable, the man who hosted the feast sent out many invitations. Those with the invitations began to make excuses that dealt with their possessions. Finally, the man sent out more invitations, but to the poor and needy who were on the streets.

You see, in the first five verses, you read about people who missed out on Jesus because they were too busy making excuses such as, "I'm too busy", or "I bought this and need to do that." There are no excuses that get you into heaven.

The parable spoke specifically about a man who bought some ground and then he was too busy to attend the feast because he now needed to inspect the land. The sin was not buying the ground; the sin was not accepting the invitation. We can get so caught up with our possessions that we lose sight of the purpose in those possessions. Having a nice home or a nice car is not a sin, but if those things control you, it becomes sin.

What are you holding onto that may be socially acceptable, but to God and your life, it's a sin?

_____

_____

Another example is Adam in Genesis. Adam didn't jump in bed with a stranger or smoke a joint. He simply disobeyed God. Yet his sin was so serious that it brought all of creation into captivity.

Tough Times Ahead

So often, we read the Bible so it pertains to our life instead of living our lives so it pertains to the Bible. Things will arise in your life even when you're sober and the natural thing to do could be the wrong thing to do. You can find comfort in knowing that if you walk in God's authority and in His obedience, no situation, person or problem can stop what God has planned in your life.

What happens when God doesn't answer your prayer as soon as you want? What will you do? Sometimes it's important for us to ask ourselves, 'Why am I in a relationship with Christ? Is it to get me out of this mess or is it because I realize I was called to serve Him with my life?'

Paul wasn't in a relationship with Christ for a miracle. Are you?

I will warn you that tough times are ahead, but this is where faith in God will carry you through.

As I said earlier, when we become a Christian, it does not mean that we miraculously become this worry-free, care-free, and problem-free person. No, we still live in this world full of sin. Therefore, we will be affected by it. Problems will arise, but it's how we handle those problems that make the difference.

Look at Abraham, for example. The first time he was blessed with land was when he lost everything, including his wife. Our hardships can be the catalyst for God's plan in our life. Abraham was a man who was the "father" of God's chosen people. Even though he was given that great title, he still had hardships ahead of him. But those hardships soon became the launching pad for the call in his life.

Jesus himself also is a great example. You read in Mathew 4, where He was tempted, yet defeated the enemy. Then the very next chapter, Matthew 5, is the beginning of his ministry. First came the hardships and then came the ministry. That is how God works.

<u>NOTES</u>

Chapter 10:
The New You

I want to tell you about a man who came through our program and graduated. I met him at a local jail through one of the classes we taught. This man was around 30, the owner of a small construction business, and extremely head strong and opinionated. He was in jail for a driving charge and was doing a few months in county. He came from a heavy drinking lifestyle. I wouldn't consider him an alcoholic, but he was addicted to the lifestyle of drinking, social drug use, and women.

During our class, he never really opened up except to argue about different things. I gave him a Bible but he never read it. However, he always attended class and I could tell he was listening. He had a mouth on him, and even though it was a faith-based course, I never felt God telling me to say anything to him about it.

Once he was released, he gave me a call and pretty much opened the door at our recovery home himself. He ended up sleeping on our couch for months because we were at capacity. He did well at the home; he was a hard worker and to be honest, I never worried about him drinking again. During this time, he was in a fight for custody of his two young boys, one of whom had a severe handicap. His baby's mom was a crack-head, and he didn't have much support from his family. However, he did well at getting his feet on solid ground, accepting Christ and getting involved in the church.

Within months, he moved out of the house to live in one of our homes with a few others, and got full custody of both of his kids. Today, he is a business owner, a man of God, and an amazing dad.

I share that story to bring up an important point. During the time at the house, he opened up about a situation that happened while he was younger. Things in our younger years affect the way we react to them 10, 20, 40 years down the road.

While this man was a young boy, around the age of seven, his brother, who was an infant, wouldn't stop crying. He would continually go to his parents, pleading with them that something was wrong with his younger brother. They never listened and played it off. Within a few days, his younger brother died of an incident that could have been prevented if his parents had taken him to the hospital when the warning signs of constant crying were happening.

At that moment, he saw his mother and father as his authority figures; authority figures who let him down. He regretted not taking things into his own hands, even though there wouldn't have been much he could do. So from that day on, he lost all respect for "authority figures" because he believed they would simply let him down, just as his parents did twenty- some years ago.

Because of his lack of respect for authority, he found himself in jail often. His problem wasn't that he enjoyed breaking the law; his problem was he didn't have proper respect for authority.

You see, the things that happen in our lives, the ways we react and the emotions and feelings we experience during them all play a huge part in the way we react to those same types of situations in the future.

Character vs. Reputation

Character is about your moral strength. Deal with the qualities inside you, believe in them, and show them in your behavior. Reputation is only about the image others see and believe about you.

> "Be more concerned about your character, than your reputation because your character is what you really are, while your reputation is merely what others think you are."
>
> -John Wooden

One of the keys to successful recovery is sharing your hardships, struggles, and victories with others. Don't fall into the "once an addict, always an addict" mentality. Christ says you're a new person. Live like it. Every day is a victory if you make it; if not, every hour or minute is.

If you had a cure for cancer, would you share it? I hope so. Crazy thing is, thousands and millions have a cure for all the world's problems (Jesus), yet very few take it to heart to share it.

I do agree that it's hard to fight a war abroad when we have a war at home. Which means, until you honestly are working on yourself and experience a little bit of victory, can you really share how glorious and victorious God can be for someone else? When people look at your life and they say, "Look at the mess you're in. You say you love God, yet your life shows nothing of the sort." What I'm saying is that we need to sweep our own house clean before we can sweep someone else's. Jesus put it this way when He said to examine the plank in our own eyes before looking for the speck of dirt in others.

A pastor once told me, "Our talk gives clarity to our walk and our walk gives credibility to our talk." This statement couldn't be more true. My belief is that we need to tell people about recovery, hope, and Jesus, but we also need to show them through our lives.

Your job is to show the world what Jesus would look like if you were a roofer, inmate, carpenter, carpet layer, lawyer or congressman, and the list goes on. That's why you were created. There is one huge story going on; the story of God. Today, will you choose to be part of it? Today, will you choose to show the world what Jesus would look like if His name was _____, from _____, _____ years old, living in the situation or job as a _____.

You won't be perfect, and you will fall at times (maybe not physically, but spiritually), **but it's not whether we fall, it's whom we fall on that makes the difference.**

Religion vs. Relationship

There are so many that are bound in legalism because they heard only the knowledge and instruction, but not the heart. I hope that you don't hear just "how to" or "do this" in this study, but learn that you hear the heart of this message.

God did not call you to religion; He called you to have a personal relationship with Him.

Let's look at Adam & Eve. God created Adam and planted two specific trees; the tree of life and the tree of the knowledge of good and evil. In Genesis 2, it says God told "him" not to eat from the tree. Personally, I believe that Adam then must have told Eve (after she was created) about not eating from the tree.

So where did they go wrong? The first problem was with communication. Second, I believe Eve (not having a personal relationship with God himself) took the knowledge secondhand from Adam. I believe that is why the serpent attacked her first and not Adam. He knew she was weaker because she didn't hear it directly from God.

In that specific story, Eve equaled religion. It was a rule, knowledge, and it came secondhand from another human's mouth. She didn't have a relationship where she heard specifically from God. When we enter that state of mind of only obeying because of a rule, we enter a danger zone spiritually. We must have a relationship with God where we freely invite Him to convict us.

Today, I get conviction over things that I never would have imagined would be a sin for myself three months ago or even three weeks ago. Things such as not eating right, manipulation, or not putting something back where I found it. Because I have a relationship with God, I can hear His conviction.

Adam and Eve lived with God and they were completely God-conscious. By taking from the fruit of the tree of knowledge of good and evil, they found a source of knowledge of what was good and evil outside of God. You see, most of us know what's right or wrong, but that knowledge in itself is religion, and it will not get us to heaven.

Remember these three things:

- God doesn't test us so He knows our heart (He already does), but so we know our heart.

- May I be before I do.

- Your intimacy with God must overshadow your service to God.

Prayer

Whether you struggle with an addiction or not, prayer is a commandment and a definite need in our lives.

Do you ever find yourself not feeling close to God? Ask yourself this question: Who moved - you or God? It's also important to remember that God is not an ATM machine. Yes, He does bless His people and heal His land. God's intention is for us to go to Him and seek His will.

2 Chronicles 7:14 states, "Then, if my people who are called by my name will humble themselves and pray and seek my face and turn from their wicked ways, I will hear from heaven and will forgive their sins and restore their land."

When was the last time you prayed, sought God's face, turned from your wicked ways and cried out to God to heal your land?

If you have ADHD like I do, then one of your struggles may be being quiet and sitting still in prayer. I finally realized that being quiet in prayer isn't about not talking; it's about listening. It is so important for us to not just rattle off all our prayers and petitions to God then leave Him hanging as He is ready to give us direction for the day. Learn to listen, which starts with being quiet.

One day, I was rattling off all my prayers to God, and in reality, forgot even who I was talking to. God smacked me in the face and spoke to my heart saying, "Look what you have done in your own power; imagine what you could do in Mine."

This shook my world and I realized that most of what I had done with the ministry, I had done in my own strength. It scared me to think about where the ministry could have been (not for my glory), but how many more lives we could have reached by now if I had only surrendered my prayer life to God.

Tell the World

Your job as an inmate, office worker, construction worker, or _____ is to show the world what Jesus Christ would look like if he was an inmate, office worker, construction worker, or _____.

We are called to love people not to change them. I have found out that the best way to love someone is to pray for him or her. Also, take the time to get to know them. Do not judge them and cast them to the swine, but show them the same grace that God showed us.

Be a witness. I am probably considered a radical Christian and I'm totally fine with that. I believe Jesus lived a radical life and we are to shadow Him, not the western civilized church.

One day, I realized that the more I am fed, the more I can feed others. I'm not speaking about food, but spiritual nourishment. I read my Bible and grow closer to God, not just for myself, but I do it so it enables me to minister to others. I realized that the more I do that, the more I can give away. Amazing, huh?

Our great commission, found in Mathew 28:16-20, states that it is not a recommendation or suggestion, but our duty to make disciples and baptize them in the name of the Father, Son and Holy Spirit. My personal opinion is that no matter how mature you are in the Lord, you should go and make disciples and minister to those around you. We are in a world of sin and sinners and we are to be the salt and light of this world.

Have a Dream

It's very important to have a passion, but it's even more important to realize that passion is usually accompanied by a burden. My passion was for those who were lost, sick, incarcerated, and hopeless. However, there were also seasons in my life where I had a passion for children, youth ministry, and the elderly.

For me one passion was from God, and the other was from seeing a need. The difference was simply the burden that came with it.

What is your passion?

_____

_____

What people group do you have a burden for?

_____

_____

Those two things usually birth the ministry that God has for you. When I first started in vocational ministry, I had a huge vision. It took years to see that start to unfold, but when times got rough, the only thing that kept me going was that vision. I would look to that for hope; it was a promise from God to me and I never lost sight of it. It might have gotten blurry at times, but I never lost sight and that's the only reason I am writing this today.

What is your vision or what can you see yourself doing (ministry-wise) for others? Think Big.

_____

_____

_____

_____

My challenge for you is to give that back to God. Tell God, "It's Yours, and it's in Your timing." I have seen ministries that God gave someone, yet they failed to give it back to God and the purpose and destiny of that ministry never reached its potential. That happened purely because they didn't take the time to give it back to God. I'll leave you with this: **busyness in serving Christ can block us from knowing Him.** What you will find is that as you help others, you're really helping yourself (step 12).

Hope-Peace-Joy-Love

This culture is losing its hearts to screens, porn, drugs, and cars. It is so easy for us, as citizens of this world, to fall into the temptations it has to offer. **Our standard cannot be the world's standard.**

We must make a decision to follow God, raise our children to know Him, and to stand up for righteousness and truth. Day in and day out, raw, straight up, you must make the decision to tend the land God placed in front of you. There will be great times, but there will also be droughts. Just remember, God not only gives you strength, but He is your strength.

When those tough times come, remember, God is willing to let our bodies suffer if it means that He will gain our hearts.

Here is a parable that rings true in my mind and life. A corn kernel, once it's planted by a seed, is grown into a corn stalk. During its short lifetime, it gets water from rain. If there is no rain, it must get it from another source. So in a time of a drought, its roots grow deeper searching for water. That way, when a storm comes and wind blows, its roots are so deep and strong, they can withhold the winds. Then it can produce what God intended it to produce.

That's our life.

So in your life, there will most likely be a time of drought. However, during that drought, don't give up; grow deeper like the corn stalk. That way when the storms of life and temptation arise in your life, your roots are deep enough to withstand the things the world throws at you. That way you can produce what you were called to produce. You can birth what God placed inside you.

The last thing I want to leave you with is hope. Hope is the reason to change. You see, God paints on a canvass much bigger than we could ever imagine. Look at the story of the disciples. They gave up everything; their reputations, possessions, family, friends, and jobs to follow this one man called Jesus Christ. Life was decent at first, but pretty soon, it took a turn. Their God, the man they gave up everything for, was beaten and tortured, crucified and died on a cross. I imagine fear swept through the hearts of those disciples. But 2000 years later, if those disciples were setting next to you, I know they would tell you that even though that day looked gloomy, in hindsight, it was the best thing that ever happened to humanity. That day, God was painting a much bigger picture than the disciples could see. Today, things may look rough for you, but persevere, and one day you will see the big picture.

The only thing that the disciples had to hold onto at the cross was hope. **Hold onto hope and never let it go.**

Please take a moment to write Rusty Boruff your questions, thoughts on the book, or to find out more on One Eighty at;

Rusty Boruff

1518 Washington Street

Davenport Iowa, 52804

Further Resources

Rusty Boruff

Rusty Boruff; author, speaker, and Founder of One Eighty.

Facebook: @rustyboruff   **Website:** www.rustyboruff.com

To receive additional resources, find out more about Rusty Boruff, or to book a training or speaking event, please visit the website.

One Eighty

Purpose: One Eighty exists to bring hope, love, and opportunity to people and communities impacted by crisis, poverty, or addiction.

Mission: One Eighty prevents crisis, poverty, and addiction before it happens, reaches out to those who are in crisis, poverty, and addiction and develops those who were in crisis, poverty, and addiction. We do this by helping people build a relationship with Jesus Christ and assisting local churches and organizations to connect with their communities.

Facebook: @180zone   **Website:** www.oneeighty.org

To receive additional resources or to find out more about One Eighty, please visit the website.

Works Cited

Alcoholics Anonymous World Services (AAWS), Alcoholics Anonymous: The Big Book. 2002.

Michael Dye and Patricia Fancher. The Genesis Process: A Relapse Prevention Workbook for Addictive/Compulsive Behaviors, 3rd ed. 2007.

A New Direction: A Cognitive Behavioral Treatment Curriculum "Intake & Orientation" Workbook. Hazelden Foundation. 2002.

A New Direction: Criminal and Addictive Thinking Workbook. Hazelden Foundation. 2002.

A New Direction: Relapse Prevention Workbook. Hazelden Foundation. 2002.

International Bible Society. The Holy Bible (NIV). Zondervan, 2005.

Additional Worksheets

The following worksheets are best done in group settings
with a teacher, counselor, or pastor.

Reacting Out of Feelings or Emotions

Behind every emotion and feeling are thoughts. Below is an exercise that focuses on rethinking through a situation that you reacted to.

My example:

Today, my baby's mom decided to change my weekend plans for my son. She said she had some things going on Saturday and Sunday. Today is Friday and now she says I can't see him. Even though she has full custody, she still needs to respect me as a parent, and he is half mine, so I should just show up and take him. I deserve him.

What emotion or feeling did you experience from this?

I was frustrated, angry, and upset. I felt disrespected and out of control.

What were the thoughts before you reacted or how did you justify your reaction?

This is dumb; I hate her, and I want my son. I haven't seen him for a week already and she has him all of the time. She probably just wants to go out with her boyfriend and sleep around. He would be better with me anyway.

What was the false belief or lie that was behind the thought?

I told myself that I have a right; however, legally I don't because she has full custody.

What was the true belief, or an alternative action you could have taken?

In Philippians, it says that once I accept Christ, I give up my "rights." I need to stop worrying because it shows a lack of trust. Maybe I do need to take the next step legally to get custody. I should have respected her authority since she is my authority in that situation (Romans 13).

When have you felt this way before?

When I was in jail, I didn't feel like I had any control. She was pregnant, and doing everything by herself, and I felt hopeless and helpless. I felt I was missing out.

Write down an event that caused you to react incorrectly.

_____

_____

What emotion or feeling did you feel from this?

_____

_____

What were the thoughts before this happened or how did you justify your reaction?

_____

_____

What was the false belief, or lie that was behind the thought?

_____

_____

What was the true belief or an alternative action you could have taken?

_____

_____

Is there another time when you have felt this way?

_____

_____

Anger

A moment of anger can change a small problem into a crisis. The only way to really control anger is to walk through it again every time it happens. Then start to re-think how you can respond to the cause. Below is a worksheet that you can use anytime that you act out in anger.

Example:

Event that caused your anger:

Speeding Ticket

Rate your anger, from 1-10 (10 being the highest):

8

Other feelings (both physical and emotional):

Fear and blood pressure raised

Justify your anger (be honest):

Wasn't fair, others were speeding, it was only 10 miles over

Un-justify your anger (be honest):

It's my fault, I was speeding

What could you have done differently?

I could have kept my cool and taken responsibility

What could the outcome be if you had acted differently?

I wouldn't have looked like an idiot and it wouldn't have ruined my day.

Your Turn:

Event that caused your anger:

_____

_____

Rate your anger, from 1-10 (10 being highest):

_____

Other Feelings (both physical and emotional):

_____

_____

Justify your anger (be honest):

_____

_____

Un-justify your anger (be honest):

_____

_____

What could you have done differently?

_____

_____

What would the outcome be if you had acted differently?

_____

_____

Conflict

Let's play a game. It's called "Name the Conflict!" Below, name the conflict then briefly write down the reason for that conflict in the last month.

Example:

Conflict:

My baby's mom and I were fighting because she was two hours late picking him up.

What was resolved? Was it worth the energy?

I kept him two hours longer, and no it wasn't.

What could you have done differently?

Spent less time complaining and more time with him.

Your Turn:

Conflict:

_____

_____

What was resolved? Was it worth the energy?

_____

_____

What could have you done differently?

_____

_____

Relationships

The number one reason that people relapse is not because of the temptation or anger. It's because of relationships. Almost all problems stem from a relationship. Anger, worry, and anxiety almost always involve someone else.

Example:

Think of the last time you used your addiction, and write it down below.

I was on a diet and have been successful at it for months. But then one day, I was at my daughter's birthday party and decided to have a piece of cake, thinking it wouldn't be a big deal. So I ate a piece of cake and pretty soon that turned into four.

What feeling did you feel?

I felt worthless and disappointed in myself. So I ended up getting off of the diet.

Where did that feeling come from, who was involved, or who caused you to feel this way?

<u>*I think it came from all the times before I failed and fell off my diet wagon. My wife was disappointed in me as well- or I perceived it that way. Didn't feel good enough to be married.*</u>

Your Turn:

Think of the last time you used your addiction and write it down below.

_____

_____

What feeling did you feel?

_____

_____

Where did that feeling come from, who was involved, or who caused you to feel this way?

_____

_____

Made in the USA
San Bernardino, CA
25 April 2016